W9-AWY-573

Florence Sabin

JUNIOR ▪ WORLD ▪ BIOGRAPHIES

Florence Sabin

ROBIN CAMPBELL

CHELSEA JUNIORS

a division of CHELSEA HOUSE PUBLISHERS

English-language words that are italicized in the text can be found in the glossary at the back of the book.

Chelsea House Publishers

EDITORIAL DIRECTOR Richard Rennert
EXECUTIVE MANAGING EDITOR Karyn Gullen Browne
COPY CHIEF Robin James
PICTURE EDITOR Adrian G. Allen
ART DIRECTOR Robert Mitchell
MANUFACTURING DIRECTOR Gerald Levine
ASSISTANT ART DIRECTOR Joan Ferrigno

JUNIOR WORLD BIOGRAPHIES
SENIOR EDITOR Martin Schwabacher
SERIES DESIGN Marjorie Zaum

Staff for FLORENCE SABIN

ASSISTANT EDITOR Catherine Iannone
COPY EDITOR William Kravitz
EDITORIAL ASSISTANT Scott D. Briggs
PICTURE RESEARCHER Villette Harris
COVER ILLUSTRATION Daniel Mark Duffy

First Printing

1 3 5 7 9 8 6 4 2

Library of Congress Cataloging-in-Publication Data

Campbell, Robin, 1937–
Florence Sabin: scientist / Robin Campbell.
p. cm.—(Junior world biographies)
Includes bibliographical references and index.
ISBN 0-7910-2291-9
1. Sabin, Florence Rena, 1871–1953—Juvenile literature. 2. Immunologists—United States—Biography —Juvenile literature. 3. Women physicians—United States—Biography—Juvenile literature. [1. Sabin, Florence Rena, 1871–1953. 2. Physicians. 3. Women—Biography.] I. Title. II. Series.
QR180.72.S23C35 1995
610'.92—dc20 94-31136
[B] CIP
AC

Contents

Acclaimed as one of the foremost medical researchers of the early 20th century, Florence Sabin valued her work above all else. After retiring from the Rockefeller Institute, she remained active in the scientific community until the age of 80.

CHAPTER

1

Honoring a Pioneer

One evening in June, 1938, Dr. Florence Sabin heard a knock at the door of her apartment in New York City. She had just gotten home from her job at the Rockefeller Institute for Medical Research, where she was the head of the Department of Cellular Studies.

Her visitors were three of her closest friends, Dr. Lawrence Kubie, Dr. Kenneth Smithburn, and Dr. Smithburn's wife, also named

Florence. They announced that they had come to take her to a special dinner.

Dr. Florence Sabin was 66 years old. After a long and successful career as a *medical researcher,* she had announced her retirement, which would take effect that December. She had decided to return to Colorado, where she would settle down with her only sister, Mary.

Her friends told her that they would celebrate her retirement at an elegant restaurant, the Rainbow Room. Dr. Sabin was overjoyed. Although she had lived in New York for 13 years, she had never been to the famous restaurant. She quickly changed into her good silk dress and Mary Jane pumps, and the four went out.

Once at Rockefeller Center, where the Rainbow Room was located, her friends played an innocent trick. Instead of going to the Rainbow Room, they brought Dr. Sabin just a floor below, to the Shell Room.

As Dr. Sabin entered the Shell Room, she was surprised to run into many of her old friends.

Then she noticed that the room was filled with *only* her friends. Suddenly she realized that she was at a party in her honor, celebrating her long years of accomplishment.

Florence Sabin was one of the first women to become a doctor in the United States, and she had had many other "firsts" in her life. She was the first woman to be chosen as a professor at Johns Hopkins School of Medicine in Baltimore, where she taught for 23 years; she was the first woman to be elected to the National Academy of Sciences, an organization of the nation's most respected scientists; and she was the first female president of the American Association of Anatomists. She had to fight *prejudice* against female scientists all her life, and at least once she was denied a job simply because she was a woman. But with hard work and determination, she managed to rise to the top of her field.

Dr. Sabin was a medical doctor, but she had decided early in her career not to be the kind of doctor who treats patients in an office or hospital.

Instead, she became a researcher and spent her life in laboratories, helping to uncover the mysteries of the human body. Her tool was not a stethoscope but a microscope.

In her early years, she had made important discoveries about the human *lymphatic system*, which is like the blood system but carries lymph, a clear fluid that bathes each *cell* of the body and cleanses the blood. She also helped scientists and doctors understand the human brain with her book *An Atlas of the Medulla and Midbrain*, which is a map of the structure of a baby's brain. Later she studied blood cells and the way they fight disease.

Dr. Sabin had had great success. But it is probable that the 40 friends who gathered at the Shell Room on that June evening were also there because of her character—her honesty, her humbleness, and her eagerness to share what she knew with her *colleagues* and students.

Sabin's friends presented her with a book in which they had recorded personal memories of her and thanked her for the influence she had had on all of them. "All blood cells love you and wish you many happy years," wrote one admirer, a reference to Dr. Sabin's work investigating the cells that make up blood. Another wrote, "You have always been my scientific godmother."

After dinner, her friends gave speeches in her honor. Dr. Kubie spoke first, reviewing Dr. Sabin's early years—her childhood in a Colorado mining town, her move to Illinois and then Vermont as a teenager, and her studies at Smith College and Johns Hopkins School of Medicine.

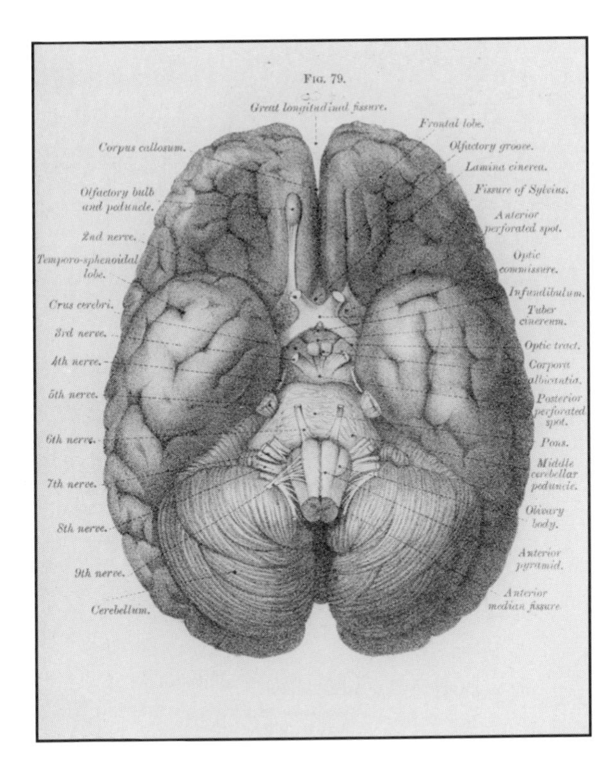

Sabin began studying the human brain while in medical school. In 1901 she published An Atlas of the Medulla and Midbrain, *which became a standard medical school textbook.*

Next, another of her friends, Dr. George Wislocki of Harvard University, rose to speak about Dr. Sabin's scientific accomplishments during the years she had taught and headed laboratories in Baltimore and New York. Because many of the guests at the party were scientists who had worked with Dr. Sabin or had been taught by her, they already knew and understood her work.

Finally, Dr. Sabin herself rose to speak. Dr. Kubie later recalled that as she spoke, it began to seem "as though this was not a dinner given in her honor. We were a group of friendly scientists gathered together to discuss things in which all were interested."

Dr. Sabin grew more and more enthusiastic as she began to describe the scientific questions she had been working on for the past few years. She also spoke about other scientists' work and how it related to hers.

At the end of her talk, still happy and enthusiastic, she announced, "the most interesting thing about it all is that in the last few weeks I have discovered that everything I have been doing in these last few years is all *wrong*."

Dr. Sabin's honest and humble character was part of what allowed her to stand up at a dinner in her honor and let everyone know that her recent theories were incorrect. But she was also able to do this because she understood how scientific investigation and discovery work.

Dr. Sabin had learned that in order to find out what is true, a researcher will sometimes spend quite a bit of time testing a *theory* that turns out to be false. Of course, she did her best to spend her time on good theories—theories that would, after experiments were done, be proved true. But being able to say what is not true, so that no one in the future will waste time exploring that possibility, is also important, and is just as much a part of the scientific process.

As Dr. Kubie put it, "The important thing in the end is the progress of knowledge and not which individual is the relay runner who for a brief span carries the torch."

Sabin decided as a teenager to pursue a career in science. As a student at the Vermont Academy, she worked hard to prepare for college.

CHAPTER

2

Colorado Childhood

Florence Rena Sabin was born in Central City, Colorado, on November 9, 1871. Central City, in Colorado's Rocky Mountains, was a mining town. It was filled with people who had come from all over the country, hoping to get rich from the gold that had been discovered in the Rockies in the late 1850s.

George Kimball Sabin, Florence's father, was one of those people. He had been in medical school in Vermont, but when he heard about the gold in Colorado he decided to move West and work in the mining business. He and a friend drove a wagon to Colorado in 1860.

Florence's mother, Serena Miner, was a schoolteacher from Vermont. As a young woman, Serena (nicknamed Rena) was always looking for new experiences, so she left home and moved to Georgia. But her life changed when the Civil War began in 1861, and a few years later the Union army marched into Georgia, burning farms and towns. Rena decided to leave the war-torn South. When she saw an advertisement for a job as a schoolteacher in Black Hawk, Colorado, she applied immediately. She got the job and took a stagecoach to Colorado. In 1868 she met George Sabin at a dance in Black Hawk, and one month later they were married.

The Sabin family lived in a wooden house perched on the side of a steep hill in Central City. One of Florence's favorite activities as a child was walking in the nearby mountains with her sister,

Mary, who was two years older than she, looking for birds and wildflowers. Florence loved the yellow flower of the prickly pear, a kind of cactus, and all her life her favorite color was yellow.

When Florence was four, the family moved to Denver, which was a larger town than Central City but not yet the big city it is today. The move made it easier for Florence's father to conduct his mining business, because he needed to travel to the various mines quite a bit and Denver was a central location.

Florence and Mary played in an empty lot across the street, where later the Denver courthouse would be built. Sometimes they ventured farther up the street to watch Arapaho and Ute Indians coming from their settlements outside of town.

The family grew in 1877, when Florence was six, with the birth of her brother Richman. But Richman died in the winter of 1877, and Florence, who felt very close to him, was deeply affected.

CHEMICALS, PAINTS, OILS, BRUSHES & GLASS.
DENVER PHOTOGRAPHIC ROOMS

Denver, Colorado, was still a frontier town with unpaved streets when the Sabins moved there in 1875.

On November 9, 1878, Florence's seventh birthday, her mother died shortly after giving birth to another child, Albert. Like Richman, Albert lived only a short time.

When Florence was young, it was much more common for women to die in childbirth and for young babies to die than it is now. Perhaps it was the sad experience of losing her mother and two brothers that helped lead Florence Sabin to her lifework—researching the causes of diseases so that they could be prevented and cured.

Their mother's death meant major changes for Florence and Mary. At first their father enrolled them at Wolfe Hall, a boarding school in Denver. He was away from Denver struggling to keep his mining business going, so they were not even able to spend Christmas together.

In the next year the Sabins' lives changed again, this time for the better. Florence and Mary went to live with their uncle Albert in Lake Forest, Illinois, on the shore of Lake Michigan. Albert, who was their father's brother, was a schoolteacher. He was married and had an 11-year-old son named Stewart.

Florence and her uncle became close. They shared a love of music and of literature. He would often take the children to orchestra concerts in nearby Chicago, and Florence learned to play the piano. Albert also shared Florence and Mary's interest in nature, and he took the children on long walks to look at plants and animals, as the girls had done in Colorado.

The relationship Florence developed with her uncle Albert would last until his death many years later. He would always be a strong supporter of her efforts in medical school and of her work as a researcher. Once when she was in medical school, she wrote to him about some *controversy* regarding her research. He wrote back, "I think you are grand. . . . You will do your whole duty as you see it. You will be serene through it all. Whether you make or break with the Faculty . . . your old Uncle will love you still and believe you are the best of the pack."

Florence and Mary lived in Lake Forest for four years, until Florence was 12. Then they moved to their grandparents' house in Vermont. There they attended the Vermont Academy, a private school nearby. When their grandmother died in 1884, the two girls briefly went back to Illinois, but they returned to the Vermont Academy in 1885.

At the Vermont Academy, Florence had her own piano, a gift from Uncle Albert, and she

After the death of their mother, seven-year-old Florence and her sister, Mary, were sent to Wolfe Hall in Denver. This photograph shows the school in 1887, a few years after the Sabins attended.

practiced with devotion. She was thinking of becoming a professional musician, but at age 16 she changed her course. It happened one day when she was practicing and some of the other girls were listening to her play, as they often did.

Florence was playing exercises and scales, and one of the listeners asked for something more fun. Florence replied that she was not playing for fun, she was working hard to become a concert pianist. The other girl told Florence that she simply did not have the talent to be a concert pianist.

Florence must have been feeling the same thing herself, because this episode convinced her to give up her hopes of being a musician. Next to music she loved science, and she decided that it was a pursuit in which she could excel.

Science was not a customary field for women at that time, but this would not stop Florence Sabin. She was elected class president the next year and graduated from the Vermont Academy with honors. And, most important, she had settled on a direction for her life.

While at Smith College, Sabin decided that she would become a doctor. She worked hard to save enough money to attend Johns Hopkins School of Medicine.

CHAPTER

3

"One in 10,000"

On a hot afternoon, September 17, 1889, Florence Sabin sat in a quiet classroom at Smith College writing busily. She and her fellow freshmen were taking the entrance examination in science.

Most of the young women knew each other, but she was a stranger, rumored to be from "out west," even though she had lived in Vermont for the past six years.

Years later, Florence Jackson, one of the other women taking the test, remembered the occasion. She recalled that Florence Sabin was wearing a blue satin shirt with a high collar and long sleeves. Jackson noted that most of the young women did not write much on the exam, "knowing little or nothing of the subjects; but the girl in the blue blouse wrote and wrote and wrote. And we realized that she was the smartest person in the room."

Smith College, in Northampton, Massachusetts, had been founded in 1871 to give women a first-rate college education. At the time, women were not allowed to attend other *prestigious* eastern colleges.

At Smith, Sabin majored in science, taking *zoology*, biology, chemistry, and geology. She also joined a group called the Colloquium—25 students who met with the science professor for discussions about scientific matters. There was some fun involved, too; the science students, for example, sometimes held tea parties in the laboratory, drinking their tea from beaker glasses and stirring it with test tubes.

At 17, Florence was a shy, bookish person, close only to her sister, Mary, who was also a student at Smith. Of short to average height, with naturally curly hair and clear blue eyes behind her glasses, Florence felt she was plain looking. Unlike some of the other women at Smith, she did not go out to parties with the men from nearby Amherst College. But it is likely that Florence did not give her appearance too much thought, since she was busy studying and deciding which branch of science she wanted to study.

Dr. Grace Preston, the school doctor and one of the country's earliest women physicians, helped Florence make this decision. Dr. Preston lived in the same boarding house as Florence and Mary, and she supported Florence in her new plan—to become a doctor. She encouraged Florence to apply to Johns Hopkins School of Medicine, which was just being established in Baltimore, Maryland.

After her third year at Smith, Florence went back to Denver to tell her father and sister about

When Sabin arrived at Johns Hopkins in 1896, the new campus had not been completed. The hospital and medical school were located in small, dingy buildings in downtown Baltimore.

ONE PRICE
& CO.
AND
SOCIETY

her plan. By this time, Mary had graduated from Smith and was working as a math teacher at Wolfe Hall, the boarding school the girls had attended long before. Mary told Florence that their father's business was not doing well and that there was not enough money for medical school.

Florence went back to Smith for her senior year determined to earn the money she needed. She tutored other students in math and history, worked in the library, and began to save.

In 1893 she graduated from Smith. She still did not have the money she would need for medical school, so she returned to her family in Denver. Like Mary, she took a job as a teacher at Wolfe Hall. She taught history, zoology, and math.

It could have been a sad period of her life, but Sabin worked hard to become a good teacher. While at Wolfe Hall, she met a friend who would be an important influence for many years to come—Ella Strong Denison. The friendship began when Sabin started taking her students on nature walks, perhaps modeled on the walks she and

Mary had taken as children in the Colorado mountains. The parents of one of the children who went on these walks mentioned them enthusiastically to Mrs. Denison, a wealthy woman who was active in the Denver schools and took an interest in education.

At the end of the term, Mrs. Denison invited Sabin to Wisconsin, where she and her children spent the summer. She wanted Sabin to instruct her two older children and two of their cousins in science and nature.

The instruction Sabin offered was not in a classroom but in the woods and fields, on nature walks. Sabin taught the children to look at things closely, noticing every detail, as scientists do. The children drew pictures of what they saw, observing such things as the number of petals on a flower, the way leaves grow on a branch, or the form of a butterfly's wings.

Sabin stayed in touch with this group of youngsters throughout her life. Theodore Sheldon, who grew up to become a lawyer in Chicago, was one of them. Years later, he still had the nature drawings he had made as a child and memories of "the inspiring and always stimulating friendship with and for our well-beloved Doctor Florence."

Ned Sheldon, who later became a well-known playwright in New York City, was another former student of Sabin's. Later in life he became ill for a long period of time, and Sabin visited him often. After one of her visits, he wrote her a note that read, "You can never know what a wonderful inspiration you are. I never came away from an evening with you without a feeling of deep joy."

Sabin's friendship with Mrs. Denison, who was 16 years older than she, was equally important. Throughout her life, Sabin would make visits to the family's home in Wisconsin, and Mrs. Denison often stayed with Sabin in New York City when Sabin lived there in later years.

Two years after graduating from Smith College, Sabin returned there in 1895 when she was offered a one-year position as a substitute professor of zoology. In 1896 she received a great honor, a summer *fellowship* to study at the Marine Biological Laboratories, a well-known research facility in Woods Hole, Massachusetts.

Sabin did not forget her desire to become a doctor, and thanks to these jobs and honors, she had been able to save the necessary money. In 1896 she applied to and was accepted at Johns Hopkins School of Medicine.

Johns Hopkins University had opened in 1876. In 1893, its School of Medicine was scheduled to open, but the school did not have enough money to begin classes. Four Baltimore women had formed the Women's Fund Committee in order to raise money for the school. They raised $500,000 but would only give it to the school if it agreed to admit women on the same basis as men. The school's president did not think that women had the same abilities as men, but he did not want to lose the support of the Women's Fund Committee, so he finally agreed to admit women to Johns Hopkins School of Medicine on "an equal basis with men."

Soon after entering medical school, Sabin began to work with a teacher who would be her strongest supporter at Johns Hopkins, and eventually one of her closest friends, Dr. Franklin Paine Mall. As a student working with him, she would do some of the most important scientific work of her entire career.

Dr. Mall, who headed the *anatomy* department, was an unusual man. In writing his biography years later, Sabin used the words "severe, critical, caustic, amusing, entertaining, and extraordinarily kindly" to describe him. "He was a

Mary Sabin graduated from Smith College two years before Florence. The sisters remained extremely close throughout their lives, even when they lived far apart.

man of power who loved to fight for ideals," she wrote, "and by sheer force of his willpower he made people go his way."

Dr. Mall believed that only one in 10,000 students had the ability to become a medical researcher. Sabin found herself completely fascinated by the work done in his lab. There she learned the many ways to stain specimens, making it easier to study their cells under a microscope. She found that she was good at the work, and Mall seemed to think she might be that special "one in 10,000." Early in Sabin's studies, he asked to see a slide she had prepared. As he looked through her microscope, he simply said, "Nice," and moved on. But from a man like Mall this was the highest praise. "It made me feel fine—as fine as silk," Sabin wrote to Mrs. Denison.

Dr. Mall encouraged Sabin to publish her first academic paper, which dealt with the nervous system. In 1897 it was featured in a respected medical journal. She was proud of her work, and she happily sent a copy of the article to her father in Colorado. But he was never able to read it, because he died suddenly in December of that year.

In spite of the shock of losing her father, Sabin continued to work hard on her research. By the end of her second year at Hopkins, she was becoming an accomplished anatomist, and Mall offered her a chance to do research on the lymphatic system. This system, similar to the blood system, bathes the body's cells and cleanses the blood. Even today it is not completely understood, though it is considered to be very important, especially in fighting disease.

After looking carefully at the slides under her microscope, Sabin found that the lymph system is connected to the blood system in a different way than scientists had previously thought. "It is an extremely small point," Mall later wrote to colleagues in Europe, "but it has caused an immense amount of trouble for the past 200 years."

Sabin would later publish several papers on the lymphatic system in medical journals. For her work in this area, she won a $1,000 prize for the best scientific paper written by a woman using new research. Some researchers consider her work on the lymphatic system to be her most important scientific contribution.

In her senior year, Sabin began a new project at Mall's suggestion. She wrote a book about the structure of the human brain. The book, *An Atlas of the Medulla and Midbrain,* became the standard textbook for medical students in this area, and it remained so for about 30 years. It can still be found in medical school libraries.

Sabin clearly was destined for a career in medical research, but as a medical student she also learned other aspects of being a doctor. Before graduating, she was required to help deliver nine babies. It gave her "a case of nerves," she said, and she wrote to Mary, "I don't seem to work well under pressure. I need a calm and placid atmosphere." She could always find that atmosphere in her laboratory, where in the coming years she would earn a reputation as one of the foremost medical researchers of her day.

After completing her medical internship, Sabin returned to Dr. Mall's laboratory. Here she is shown with Johns Hopkins professor William Osler (second from right) and two colleagues.

CHAPTER 4
Fighting the Odds

Sabin graduated from medical school in 1900, third in her class. During their years at Johns Hopkins, she and the other female students had endured pranks and jokes from the male medical students and sometimes from the professors. But now the *discrimination* took a more serious turn.

The next step for the graduates was an internship. During an internship, medical school graduates work in a hospital, where they are supervised and trained by experienced doctors. At Johns Hopkins, four internships were available in medicine, four in surgery, and four in gynecology. The best students would be offered the internships in medicine. Of the top students, one man had to drop out because of ill health, and one chose a surgery internship. That left Sabin at the head of the list. Another woman, Dorothy Reed, came in fourth.

The directors of the hospital did not want to give two of the four most important internships to women, so they asked Dorothy Reed if she would take an internship in surgery or gynecology instead. She refused.

Sabin at first offered to take a fellowship in anatomy and allow Reed to have the medicine internship. But after talking it over, the two women agreed that they would take what they were entitled to, rather than be denied simply because they were women. When faced with the women's determination, the directors decided to award both Sabin and Reed the prestigious medical internships.

After the yearlong internship, Sabin again faced the possibility of being denied a post simply because she was a woman. She was eligible to become a doctor at the Johns Hopkins Hospital, but the hospital did not allow women on its staff.

The Women's Fund Committee, which continued to look after the female medical students, planned to help Sabin challenge the hospital, but Dr. Mall intervened. He offered her a one-year fellowship to work as a researcher in his laboratory. The Women's Fund Committee raised the money to pay Sabin a salary.

During the next year, Sabin continued her work on the lymphatic system, and her discoveries began to become more widely known. Her work was considered important enough in 1903 that she was offered the job of assistant professor in the anatomy department, even though the school had never before hired a female professor.

Sabin had always loved sharing her knowledge with others, so she was happy to be teaching and supervising students in their research. Better still, as a professor of anatomy she would continue working with Mall.

Ever since her work at Wolfe Hall, Sabin had taken seriously the job of teaching. Her mentor, Dr. Mall, did the same. As Sabin began teaching at Hopkins, Mall told her, "Above all, do not make your teaching so rigid that you rob the students of the pleasure of discovering things for themselves." But she did not believe in making things too easy. "It's dishonest," she once said, "to simplify anything that isn't simple."

Sabin also believed that students could learn more from their own experiments and observations than from books. She once said, "Books are mere records of what other people have thought and observed. The material is a much more accurate guide." Similarly, Dr. Mall had a sign hanging in his anatomy lab that read, "Your Body Is Your Textbook."

Sabin wanted to be sure that her classes were always fresh and interesting, so she tore up the notes to each lecture she gave after she was done. This way, she would not be tempted to read the same thing to her students each year but would have to rethink and reresearch the material to be sure it was up to date.

Sabin's enthusiasm was noted by many of her students, and it was said she could often be seen bent over her microscope late into the night. She later recounted that the most exciting experience of her life took place in the lab late one night, when under her microscope she watched the birth of the blood system of a chicken embryo (a chick that is developing inside an egg). First she saw the blood vessels form, then the cells from which red and white blood cells are made, and finally the heart, with its first beat.

Sabin taught at Johns Hopkins School of Medicine for 22 years; shown here is the new campus as it looked in 1910.

But work was not Sabin's only pleasure, although she had once said that work and sleep were her only necessities. At this point in her life she began to add a third necessity—friends.

One of Sabin's first close friends in Baltimore was Mabel Mall, Dr. Mall's wife. Mabel Mall also had been a medical student, but she had dropped out in the first year to marry her professor. In that era, no one thought a woman could be both a wife and a medical student.

Sabin enjoyed visiting the Mall home, especially after the Malls had children. One of these children, Margaret Mall Vignoles, wrote to Sabin on her 80th birthday, saying that Sabin was probably her oldest friend—because their friendship began when Margaret was only three weeks old. "I have always loved you in a very special way as a member of the Mall family," she wrote.

Sabin wrote to Margaret that she vividly remembered feeling "overwhelmed with joy" upon visiting Mabel after Margaret was born.

"Your mother was still in bed (not like the modern mother, up and downtown shopping) and looked very beautiful under one of the camel's hair blankets which you and I love," she wrote. "How amazingly my life has been enriched by having been 'taken into the Mall family,' and how your letter brought it all back to me."

Another close friend was Edith Houghton Hooker, who also had been a medical student but had quit when she married fellow medical student Donald Hooker. She and her husband worked to improve *public health,* and they founded a home for unmarried mothers in Baltimore.

Edith Hooker and Mabel Mall were also active in the movement to win the right to vote for women. Though she was a doctor making important discoveries about the human body, Florence Sabin was not allowed to cast a vote to choose the government under which she lived. Women in the United States were not given the right to vote until 1920, 20 years after Sabin became a doctor.

Sabin's research kept her busy, but she felt that it was important to donate some of her time to the *suffrage* movement. She began to support a local suffrage group by writing letters to congressmen and marching in parades in Baltimore and Washington, D.C. But the other members of the group encouraged Sabin to concentrate on her research. They believed that she could help women more by gaining respect as a scientist and encouraging other women to study science and medicine. As her career took more of her time, she became less active in the suffrage movement, but Sabin never lost interest in the struggle for women's rights. She helped her friends Edith and Mabel publish a weekly newsletter, the Maryland *Suffrage News.* In the 1920s she bought her first car and named it the *Susan B. Anthony,* after the famous crusader for voting rights.

Florence Sabin's ideas about women's rights were not simple. Despite the problems she faced with the people in power at Hopkins, she usually did not want to make a fuss—as in the case of the internship, when at first she was willing to take another appointment to avoid controversy.

However, she once praised another female doctor as "a gentle lady and a practical idealist who could survive the bitter pioneering days of women in medicine." The word "bitter" gives some idea of her feelings about the environment in which she had struggled for her achievements. And the phrase "practical idealist" describes her own attitude about surviving in such an environment: she believed that she could get what she wanted in her career by working hard and proving herself to be an outstanding scientist.

Despite her activities in the suffrage movement, Edith Houghton Hooker had time to run a busy household, of which Sabin was often a member. Donald and Edith had eight children, and there were always between five and ten dogs. Sabin spent every Christmas with them for many years.

Sabin always enjoyed the company of children, and she was very caring with them. There is a story that once, when a colleague fainted at a meeting, Sabin rushed to his home to reassure his children about what had happened. To calm the fears of the younger ones, she gave a demonstration of fainting so they would know what it was.

After she became a professor, Sabin was finally able to afford her own apartment. For several years she had shared a home with Gabrielle Clements, an art teacher. Sabin had always been interested in art and music, and her 40-year friendship with Clements gave her a chance to learn more about painting, drawing, and sculpture.

In the early part of the century, the writer Gertrude Stein was a medical student at Johns Hopkins. She lived in Baltimore with her brother Leo, who was already beginning the art collection that would become famous in Paris in the 1920s. Stein was a failure as a medical student, but she and Sabin became, and remained, friends. Florence, Gertrude, and Leo would sometimes go to the opera together, and the Steins often attended Sabin's dinner parties.

During the school year, Dr. Sabin was busy

In this 1914 photograph, a group of suffragettes campaign for women's voting rights. Although Sabin was breaking ground for women scientists, she would not be given the right to vote until 1920.

working in her lab and teaching. But during the summers she began to travel to Europe, sometimes for pleasure and sometimes combining study with her vacation. Before World War I began in 1914, she made many trips to the University of Leipzig in Germany, and she also traveled to France and Italy. On some trips her sister, Mary, went along, and once she brought the daughter of Carla Denison, one of the children she had taken on nature walks in Wisconsin before she entered medical school.

Sabin also began to win honors during this time in her life. In 1910 she was awarded an honorary doctorate of science from Smith College. Honorary doctorates are awards given by colleges each year to people of great achievement. During her lifetime, Dr. Sabin received 17 such degrees from various schools.

But in spite of these honors, Sabin continued to face discrimination at Hopkins. In 1917, Dr. Mall died after a gallbladder operation. Sabin had worked with him for 20 years, and she was the logical choice to fill his post as *chair* of the anatomy department. But Hopkins had never appointed a woman as chair of a department, and Mall's anatomy department was considered the most important in the school. In the end, the job was given to a man who had been taught by Sabin.

Sabin's students planned a *demonstration* against the appointment. Sabin was extremely disappointed at being denied the job, but she did not want to create a controversy, so she told her students to call off the demonstration. When asked if she would stay at Hopkins despite being passed over for this important job, she replied, "Of course I'll stay. I have research in progress."

The school tried to make peace with Sabin by making her the chair of another department. This position was not as prestigious as the one in the anatomy department, but it made Sabin the first woman to become a full professor at Johns Hopkins.

It was clear that Sabin was rising to the top of her field when, in 1925, she became the first woman elected to the National Academy of Sciences. Johns Hopkins released this publicity photograph to celebrate her achievement.

CHAPTER

5

Years of Distinction

In 1922, Sabin traveled to Peking, China. By this time, she had begun to research the various kinds of white blood cells, and the Peking Medical Union invited her to give a speech about her work. She also advised the Chinese government on how to control malaria—a disease that was killing many people in China at the time.

Since Sabin had learned about Asian art from some of her artist friends, she took this opportunity to acquire several valuable Chinese paintings. Gertrude and Leo Stein were interested in the artwork, and they gave Sabin advice on adding to her collection of Asian art, which would continue to grow throughout her life.

That same year, Sabin had the honor of introducing the famous French scientist Marie Curie when she spoke to the American Association of University Women. Marie Curie and her husband Pierre had been awarded the Nobel Prize for physics in 1903. Marie was a professor of physics at the Sorbonne in Paris, and in 1911 she won the Nobel Prize in chemistry. Her success inspired Sabin and other female scientists.

In 1924, Sabin was named president of the American Association of Anatomists, and in 1925 she was elected to the National Academy of Sciences. In both cases, she broke new ground for women.

Dr. Sabin received another honor in 1925, when she was offered a position at the Rockefeller Institute for Medical Research in New York City. She was asked to lead its Department of Cellular

Studies. Although she felt attached to Baltimore, where she had lived for 28 years, she decided to make the change.

The Rockefeller Institute for Medical Research, where Sabin was to work until she retired, was founded by the millionaire John D. Rockefeller in 1901. One of his advisers had read a book by a Johns Hopkins doctor who stated that cures for diseases could be found if money was put into medical research. Rockefeller was convinced, and he put $250,000—a large sum in those days—into founding the institute.

Dr. Simon Flexner, who had been Sabin's teacher at Hopkins, was the director of the institute. The board of directors instructed him to hire the best scientists to run the departments. "Only a genius is worth a laboratory wing," one member told him. Dr. Flexner believed that Sabin fit that description.

Sabin wanted her lab in New York to be like the labs that Dr. Mall had set up at Johns Hopkins—it had to be bright, sunny, and most important, perfectly clean. She always washed her hands between each stage of an experiment and before leaving or entering the lab. Now she could make this rule for everyone working under her.

Yet the lab was a friendly place. One of her co-workers later remembered, "She was nearly always the first one at the laboratory, and greeted every one with a *joie de vivre* [joy in living] which started the day pleasantly for all of us."

In this period of her life, Sabin continued to concentrate on studying white blood cells, specifically the kind called monocytes. White blood cells are important in fighting disease. Sabin was especially interested in finding a cure for *tuberculosis*, which at that time was a deadly and fairly common illness.

In 1926, Sabin joined the research committee of the National Tuberculosis Association, which hoped to keep track of all research on tuberculosis done in the United States so that information, money, and laboratories could be shared. In the 1920s tuberculosis was the number one cause of death in the United States. By 1960, it had dropped to number 18. Sabin's efforts were part of this victory.

Another part of Sabin's work involved antibodies, substances that the body produces to fight disease. At the Rockefeller Institute, she developed the theory that antibodies were produced in monocytes, but she continued until her retirement in 1938 to try to understand exactly what antibodies are. Even today, many of these questions remain

Albert Einstein's theories revolutionized the field of physics. Meeting such eminent scientists as Einstein and Marie Curie was one of the rewards of Sabin's career.

unanswered. As it turned out, finding effective medicines to fight tuberculosis was possible without understanding monocytes or antibodies.

Sabin knew that scientific research does not always produce dramatic results. The progress of medicine is the slow and steady gathering of more and more information about the complex and mysterious human body. "Everyone knows," she once said, "that I have no patience with those who think that each new idea is a 'King Strike.'"

Her research and the warm personal relationships made in connection with her work were the most important things in Sabin's life in New York, as they had been in Baltimore. Many of her co-workers praised the atmosphere she developed in her lab at the Rockefeller Institute. As one of her secretaries put it, "Somehow 'the chief' makes us feel so congenial and safe."

Life outside the lab also continued to be rewarding. One evening in the early 1930s, Sabin had the opportunity to sit next to Albert Einstein at a dinner party given by Dr. Flexner. She later said that Einstein was "utterly simple, as all great thinkers are." And she wrote to her sister, Mary, "His laugh rings out and makes everyone around him happy."

Sabin continued to win honors, both in her field and in the wider world. *Pictorial Review* magazine awarded her $5,000 for "the most distinctive contribution made by an American to American life in the field of art, science, and letters." In 1931 she was named one of America's 12 most eminent living women by *Good Housekeeping* magazine. And she was awarded honorary degrees by several universities.

Through these years, Sabin continued to believe that work, sleep, and friends were the three things she needed for a happy life—with work perhaps chief among them. One evening at a New York dinner party, she was heard to say, "It is now night, and I am glad. For soon morning will come and I can again open the door of my beloved laboratory."

Sabin retired from the Rockefeller Institute in 1938, but her career was far from over. When scientists at the University of Colorado asked for her assistance with their research on white blood cells, Sabin, now in her seventies, was happy to be back at work.

CHAPTER

6

Public Health Reformer

In 1938, Sabin was 66 years old. She was as interested as ever in her research and felt she was on the verge of a major discovery. But she thought she should consider retiring. Her sister, Mary, agreed, writing, "You and I have not been together for Thanksgiving since 1894 . . . nor on Christmas since 1897." She wanted Florence to return to Colorado, where they would live together.

That urging, and several bouts with pneumonia, were not enough to compel Sabin to leave her "beloved laboratory." But because of the Rockefeller Institute's retirement policies, Sabin was more or less required to leave. Mary responded, "It's high time you resigned."

Mary and Florence had stayed almost as close as they had been as children facing the world together after the death of their mother. They wrote each other often, filling their letters with the daily details of their lives. Mary had retired from her work as a schoolteacher in 1931. She had lived in Colorado almost all her life, and like Florence had never married. An avid mountain climber, Mary had published a series of articles on climbing in the *Rocky Mountain News* in 1911, and she was a founding member of the Colorado Mountain Club in 1912. She also loved to travel and went to Alaska by herself in 1935, after Florence said she could not leave her work to go with her.

Sabin moved to Colorado, and she and Mary began planning activities and trips to fill their retirement years. But Sabin missed New York and her work. She began to make trips back to her lab to work on ideas or attend meetings. On one such trip she wrote to Mary, "I am back with good newspapers, soft water and work."

On another occasion, she wrote to Mary very excited about her new discoveries: "I have had wonderful talks with people here about my new theory—and I think it will stir up quite a lot of new work. I am sorry to have been away so long, but you see I could not help it."

Sabin also kept busy in Colorado, writing papers and giving talks. But she grew tired of traveling between New York and Colorado, and she began to feel that she was working on too many different projects. This changed in 1944, near the end of World War II, when Colorado governor John Vivian began forming his Post-War Planning Committee. Frances Wayne, a reporter for the *Denver Post,* asked the governor if there would be any women on the committee. She suggested Florence Sabin.

Governor Vivian was afraid of losing the support of women voters, so he agreed to appoint a woman to the committee. He did not want to address Colorado's health problems, so he was hoping to appoint someone who would not fight for change. Sabin's age and her shyness fooled the governor into thinking that she would not make any trouble for him by bringing up difficult issues. One adviser said, "We aren't worried about her—she's too old to be of any force." So Sabin was appointed to head the subcommittee on health. The governor would soon realize that in spite of her humble personality, Florence Sabin had a strong will and was determined to improve health conditions in her home state.

Her work on the Post-War Planning Committee gave Sabin the focus she had been missing since her retirement. Over the next five years, Sabin, now in her seventies, was a whirlwind of political activity. She had spent her life looking through microscopes, but she had also learned to work with all sorts of people. Now she was ready to fight for, and win, improvements in the public health laws of Colorado.

Health conditions in Colorado were not good. The death rate in Colorado was twice as high as in other states. In some places, mothers would not give their children milk to drink because it was too dirty. In one town Sabin visited, she asked her guide to show her the sewage treatment plant, where sewage is processed so that it can be released into the environment in a safe form. The guide's husband said, "Take her down to the river"—where raw sewage was being dumped. Many diseases were being spread by the sewage.

Sabin knew that many deaths could be prevented by good public health practices. New laws needed to be passed, since Colorado's health laws had been written in 1876 and much had been learned since then about what was necessary to prevent deaths.

But before new laws could be approved, Sabin had to win the support of the public. She traveled to all parts of Colorado to hold public meetings. In Denver she invited influential farmers, business people, and legislators to a series of dinners at a famous hotel. In each case, she tried to educate people about the problems and then get them fired up to do something about them.

Sabin was especially concerned about a disease that was passed to people through the milk and meat produced by sick cattle. She wanted to control the disease by passing the Cow Health Bill, which would require farmers to keep their cattle free of the illness. People in the meat and dairy

industries were opposed to the bill. They thought that they would have to spend a lot of money to keep the animals healthy. Sabin traveled throughout the state talking to cattle farmers. She explained that healthy cattle produce more milk and meat, so the Cow Health Bill would actually help the farmers make more money. She eventually won their support, and the bill was passed.

Before the new laws were drawn up, Dr. Carl Buck was hired to study the state's health problems. Sabin heard that his report "was going

Cattle raising is an important part of Colorado's economy. Sabin traveled throughout the state to win cattle farmers' support for the Cow Health Bill, which would prevent the spread of disease from cattle to people.

to be put in a desk drawer and locked up" so that no one would have to act on the problems it uncovered. So she had 1,000 copies of the Buck report made, and she distributed them to every influential person she could find. "It's hard to get 1,000 copies into a desk drawer," she commented.

Sabin loved these years of hard work and accomplishment. She once ran into a friend in a hallway and reported, "I've just been having a fight with the Civil Service Commission, and it was wonderful."

Sabin was so successful in winning the support of the people of Colorado that in the 1946 election, every official who had opposed her public health bills was voted out of office, including Governor Vivian. In 1947, six major bills were introduced in the state legislature, and most of them were passed.

Sabin was then appointed by the mayor of Denver to chair the city's health department. She began a program to test people for tuberculosis using X rays. After two years, the rate of tuberculosis in Denver had been cut in half. She also focused on hospital and restaurant cleanliness and on the rats that swarmed in the alleys of Denver.

In 1951, Sabin decided that she could no longer devote her time to improving public health. She had a more urgent concern—the health of her sister. Mary, at the age of 82, was very ill and needed constant care. Sabin, who at 80 was ready at last to retire, did not want to put her sister in a nursing home, so she decided to give up her work and take care of Mary herself.

Throughout her busy career, Sabin had tried to keep up her other interests, and in her "second retirement" she had time to do so. She became interested, for example, in the theory that Shakespeare did not write the plays attributed to him—so she reread all of Shakespeare.

Dr. Lawrence Kubie, who had spoken at the party for her "first retirement" when she left New York, visited her in Denver. He found her sitting with a blanket over her knees, a bowl of red roses on the table, and books nearby, one about Shakespeare, one by Albert Einstein, and one by her old friend Leo Stein.

"I've been thinking," she said, "about human nature, and about how hard it is to be a human being."

And yet judging by the speeches given at her 80th birthday party, Florence Sabin had gained the respect of her friends and colleagues by being not only a brilliant scientist but also a generous and caring human being. Dr. Alfred Cohn commented on why she had been so successful. "It has been, I think, because of your great humanity," he said. "You have cared deeply for your kind." He called her "a rare total person . . . [with] heart and mind in just and balanced union."

"Your scientific discoveries I have witnessed with zest and admiring delight," said Dr. Peyton Ross in his speech, "but your lessons of how to do and what to be have gone more deeply home. . . . No longer do we hail you as a great woman, but as a great and kind human being."

Sabin was honored by the University of Colorado in December 1951 when it dedicated the Florence Rena Sabin Building for Research in Cellular Biology. The following year, the American Association of University Women established the Florence R. Sabin Fellowship, which would be awarded to other women who did valuable work in the area of public health.

Sabin soon found that caring for Mary was a strain on her own health. She again came down with pneumonia, and while she was in the hospital, Mary had to move into a nursing home.

When Sabin came home from the hospital, she needed around-the-clock nursing care. On the first Sunday in October, 1953, she and her nurse sat watching the World Series on television. The New York Yankees were beating Sabin's favorite team, the Brooklyn Dodgers. When Dr. Sabin stood for the seventh-inning stretch, she fell to the floor. She had died suddenly of a heart attack at the age of 81.

Her funeral was held in Denver, and many eminent people made speeches in her honor. But as Mark Harrington—who had worked with her in her fight to improve public health in Colorado—said, "Dr. Sabin needs no commendation, for nobleness of spirit, sincerity of purpose and unremitting effort have their own reward."

Florence Sabin, who above all valued "unremitting effort" to achieve the goals she set, and who strove to embody the nobility of the human spirit, would have appreciated those words.

This painting of Dr. Sabin hangs at the University of Colorado, which also honored her by dedicating the Florence Rena Sabin Building for Research in Cellular Biology.

Further Reading

Bryan, Jenny. *Health and Science.* Women History Makers Series. New York: Watts, 1988.

Haber, Louis L. *Women Pioneers of Science.* New York: Harcourt Brace Jovanovich, 1979.

Hume, Ruth. *Great Women of Medicine.* New York: Random House, 1964.

Phelan, Mary Kay. *Probing the Unknown: The Story of Dr. Florence Sabin.* New York: Crowell, 1969.

Ranahan, Demerris. *Contributions of Women: Medicine.* Minneapolis: Dillon, 1981.

Veglahn, Nancy. *Women Scientists.* New York: Facts on File, 1992.

Glossary

anatomy a branch of science that deals with the structure of the body

cells the tiny building blocks that make up all living things; cells are so small that they can only be seen under a microscope

chair a person who heads a department or organization

colleague a person with whom one works, or a member of the same profession

controversy a disagreement that often causes tension between groups of people with different opinions

demonstration a public gathering of a group of people that is meant to show how they feel about something, usually in protest

discrimination treating a group of people unfairly because of **prejudice** against their gender, race, ethnic background, or other factors

fellowship a position in which a student receives money from a university or other organization to allow her to study or do research

lymphatic system a system of the human body that is similar to the blood system but carries lymph, which cleanses all the cells of the body

medical researcher a scientist who makes observations and does experiments in order to learn new things about the human body and how to keep it healthy

prejudice a negative opinion of a group of people that has been formed without any real knowledge of those people

prestigious well known and respected

public health the science of preventing the spread of disease and improving health conditions of an entire community

suffrage the right to vote

theory an idea that is tested through experiments

tuberculosis a contagious disease that usually affects the lungs; tuberculosis was a leading cause of death until the middle of the 20th century

zoology a branch of science that deals with animals

Chronology

Nov. 9, 1871	Florence Rena Sabin is born in Central City, Colorado.
1893	Graduates from Smith College and returns to Colorado to earn money for medical school.
1896	Enters Johns Hopkins School of Medicine and begins studying with Dr. Franklin Paine Mall.
1900	Sabin graduates from medical school.
1901	Sabin's *Atlas of the Medulla and Midbrain* is published and becomes a standard medical school textbook.
1903	Johns Hopkins School of Medicine hires Sabin as assistant professor of anatomy.
1917	Sabin's mentor Franklin Mall dies; Sabin is appointed full professor, making her the first female professor at Johns Hopkins; begins research on white blood cells.

1924 Becomes the first female president of the American Association of Anatomists.

1925 Becomes the first woman to be elected to the National Academy of Sciences; moves to New York to work at the Rockefeller Institute for Medical Research.

1938 Retires and moves to Colorado to live with her sister, Mary.

1944 Appointed head of a state subcommittee on health; travels throughout the state to gain support for new laws to improve health conditions.

1947 Most of Sabin's public health bills are passed by the Colorado legislature; Sabin is appointed chair of Denver's health department and leads a campaign to test people for tuberculosis.

1951 Gives up her work to care for Mary; the University of Colorado dedicates the Florence Rena Sabin Building for Research in Cellular Biology.

Oct. 3, 1953 Florence Sabin dies.

Index

Robin Campbell has a bachelor's degree in history from the University of Illinois and a master's degree in journalism from Northwestern University. She has worked as a newspaper reporter in California, Maine, and Wisconsin. Currently she is a medical transcriptionist in Cheboygan, Wisconsin, and in her spare time works on poetry, novels, and a vintage race car.

Picture Credits

The Bettmann Archive: pp. 48–49, 66–67; The Alan Mason Chesney Medical Archives of the Johns Hopkins Medical Institutions: pp. 43, 52 (Doris Day) Colorado Department of Public Health and Environment: p. 60; Colorado Historical Society: pp. 6, 14, 22, 38; Denver Public Library, Western History Department: pp. 18–19; Historical Division, Cleveland Medical Library Association: p. 11; Maryland Historical Society: pp. 28–29; Sophia Smith Collection, Smith College, Northampton, MA: pp. 24, 34; University of Colorado, Health Sciences Center: p. 2; University of Colorado at Boulder, Office of Public Relations: p. 72; UPI/Bettmann: p. 57.